W9-CAE-976

An Online Visit to
EUROPE

File Edit View Go Bookmarks Communicator Help

Back Forward Reload Home Search Images Print Security Stop

Netsite:

Erin M. Hovanec

The Rosen Publishing Group's
PowerKids Press™
New York

For my Mom, Mary Ellen Hovanec

Published in 2001 by The Rosen Publishing Group, Inc.
29 East 21st Street, New York, NY 10010

Copyright © 2001 by The Rosen Publishing Group, Inc.

All rights reserved. No part of this book may be reproduced in any form without permission in writing from the publisher, except by a reviewer.

First Edition

Book Design: Maria Melendez

Photo Credits: Cover, title page, Child in Bavarian Dress © Adam Woolfitt/CORBIS; title page, Reindeer © Michael S. Yamashita/CORBIS; title page, Tower Bridge, London © Johnny Stockshooter/International Stock; title page, eagle, black bear, and badger © Digital Stock; p. 7 (Parthenon) © Damm/Zefa/H. Armstrong Roberts; p. 8 (Red Square) © Dean Conger/CORBIS; p. 11 (St. Peter's Square and Basilica) © Vittoriano Rastelli/CORBIS; p. 12 (The Alps in Winter) © Karl Weatherly/CORBIS; p. 15 (Reindeer in Woods) © Tim Thompson/CORBIS; p. 16 (Dutch girl) © Chad Ehlers/International Stock; p. 19 (automobile assembly line) © Bavaria/H. Armstrong Roberts; p. 20 (Louvre, Paris) © Hilary Wilkes/International Stock.

Hovanec, Erin M.
     An online visit to Europe / Erin M. Hovanec.
        p. cm.— (Internet field trips)
     Includes index.
     Summary: An online trip to various internet web sites reveals a variety of facts about the continent of Europe, a continent that 730 million people call home.
     ISBN 0-8239-5657-1
     1. Europe—Computer network resources—Juvenile literature. 2. Europe—Computer network resources—Directories—Juvenile literature. 3. Web sites—Directories—Juvenile literature. [1. Europe.] I. Title. II. Series.

D907.H68 2000
025.06'94—dc21   00-039169

Contents

Start "Surfing" the Internet

You can visit Europe by "surfing" the Internet at home, at your school or at a public library. Here's what you will need:

A personal computer

A personal computer is necessary. If you don't have one at home, go online at your school or public library.

A modem

You'll also need a modem. This device connects you to a telephone line and to other computers.

A telephone connection

Your modem talks to other computers through a telephone line.

Internet software

To get started, you'll also need Internet software. Software tells your computer how to use the Internet.

An Internet Service Provider

An Internet Service Provider (ISP) will allow you to surf the Net for a small monthly fee.

Back Forward Reload Home Search Images Print Security Stop

Netsite: What's Related

Let's Take a Trip Online!

Would you like to travel through Europe, visiting England, Spain, Germany and many other countries? You can visit Europe on the Internet. The Internet is a network of computers that are connected to one another. People call this connection the "World Wide Web," the "Net," or the "Web." It's possible to find tons of free and fun information on the Internet by using a search engine. A search engine is a computer program that has millions of pieces of information. Type in the word "Europe" and you will see a list of colored hyperlinks on your screen. Click on a hyperlink and you will be connected to a Web page about Europe.

5

Netsite: What's Related

Tour Europe Online

Europe is one of Earth's seven **continents**. Unlike most of the other continents, Europe isn't a separate body of land. It is the western part of a huge **landmass** that makes up Europe and Asia. Europe is bordered by water on three sides. To its north is the Arctic Ocean. To its west is the Atlantic Ocean. The large body of water to its south is the Mediterranean Sea. Europe is the second smallest continent. It is about four million square miles (10.4 million sq km) in size. Despite its small size, 730 million people call Europe home, giving it the second-highest **population** of the seven continents. That's more than twice as many people as in North America!

6

The Parthenon in Athens, Greece, was built about 2,400 years ago to honor the Greek goddess Athena. It was built on an acropolis, one of the highest points in Athens.

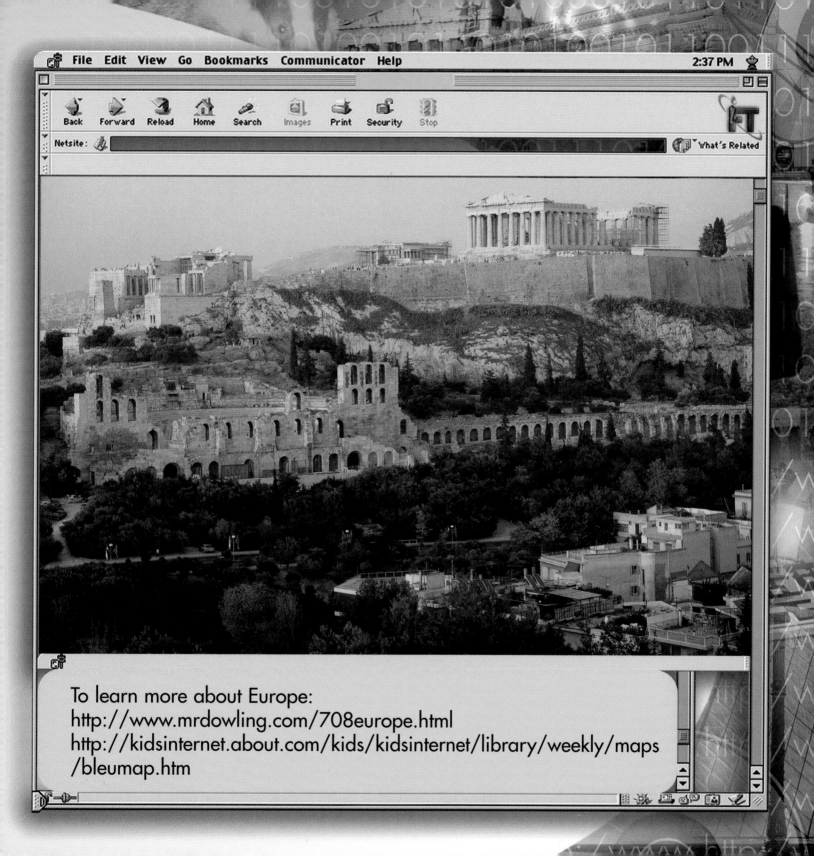

To learn more about Europe:
http://www.mrdowling.com/708europe.html
http://kidsinternet.about.com/kids/kidsinternet/library/weekly/maps
/bleumap.htm

To learn more about weather and climate:
http://www.kidsdomain.com/kids/links/Weather.html
http://cbc.ca/weather/europe.html
http://nws-sc.wctp.noaa.gov/Office/kidsweather/index.html

File   Edit   View   Go   Bookmarks   Communicator   Help   2:37 PM

Back   Forward   Reload   Home   Search   Images   Print   Security   Stop

Netsite: What's Related

What Kind of Climate?

Are you wondering what the weather is like in Europe today? Chances are it's probably pretty nice. In general Europe has a moderate **climate**. It's not always cold and snowy like Antarctica or hot and wet like South America. Different areas in Europe have different climates. Southern European countries, like Italy and Greece have dry, hot summers. Northern European countries, such as parts of Russia, have very cold winters and mild summers. The average winter temperature in Moscow, Russia, is 14 degrees Fahrenheit (-10° C). That's cold! The average winter temperature in Greece is 46 degrees Fahrenheit (8° C). Where would you like to spend the winter?

◀ *Moscow, Russia, has some of the coldest winters in Europe. This photo shows people in Moscow's Red Square, with St. Basil's Cathedral in the background.*

9 ▶

HONY CREEK LIBRARY
1350 GREENFIELD PIKE
NOBLESVILLE, IN 46060

Countries Big and Small

Europe contains more individual countries than any other continent. There are over 40 in all! These include countries such as Sweden, Belgium, Poland, Germany, and Portugal. Some countries are actually large islands. They include Great Britain and Iceland. You can find both the largest and the smallest countries in the world in Europe. Russia, the largest country on Earth, is 6.6 million square miles (17 million sq km). Russia is so big, that part of it is on the continent of Asia. Almost 150 million people live there. Vatican City in Italy is the world's smallest country. It is only one-fifth of a mile (.322 km) in size. About 1,000 people live there.

10

People from all over the world visit St. Peter's Square in Vatican City.

For more information about Europe's countries:
http://www.lonelyplanet.com/dest/loc-eur.htm
http://www.geographia.com/indx03.htm
http://www.odci.gov/cia/publications/factbook/figures/802637.jpg

For more information about the Alps and Venice:
http://alps.virtualave.net/
http://www.niksula.cs.hut.fi/~vka/Alps95/index.html
http://www.iuav.unive.it/~juli/venindx.html

Something for Everyone

There are so many amazing places to see in Europe. Europe contains many mountain ranges. The most famous are the Alps, which run through France, Italy, Switzerland, Germany, Austria, and Slovenia. In the snowy Alps, you'll find some of the tallest and the most spectacular mountains in the world. If you prefer warm weather and the seaside, head to southern Europe. Greece is famous for its beaches of white, red, and even black sand. For a unique adventure, take an online trip to Venice, Italy. This ancient city is built on the water and along **canals**. To get from place to place, people travel by boat through the canals.

This is a photo of the Alps in Courmayeur, near Mont Blanc. Mont Blanc borders France, Italy, and Switzerland.

13

Bears, Badgers,
AND WILD BOARS

Have you ever seen a reindeer? Flocks of them can be found in Lapland, a far-northern region of Europe. The mountains and forests of Europe are perfect homes for many furry animals. You'll find bears, elk, foxes, and wolves. Badgers, hedgehogs, and wild boar also call Europe home. Seals play off European coastlines, and fish, like anchovy, cod, and salmon, live in the waters there. Birds, such as eagles, owls, nightingales, and storks live in Europe, too. Once many more animals lived in Europe. Now that so many people live there, animals have less room to roam. People in Europe are working to protect animals and to keep them from becoming **extinct**.

14

These reindeer live in Lapland. Lapland is a region that lies in the far north of Norway, Sweden, Finland, and Russia.

To learn more about Europe's reindeer and other animals:
http://versaware.animalszone.lycos.com/continents/europe.asp
http://www.geocities.com/EnchantedForest/Cottage/7734/europe.html
http://www.bearcountryusa.com/animals/reindeer.htm

To learn more about the people who live in Europe:
http://wfs.vub.ac.be/cis/festivals
http://www.Searcheurope.com

Back　Forward　Reload　Home　Search　Images　Print　Security　Stop

Netsite:　　　　　　　　　　　　　　　　　　　　　　What's Related

Proud Peoples of Europe

Europe contains many different ethnic groups. Groups such as the British, Dutch, and Polish people all have their own history, lifestyle, religion, and language. More than 50 languages are spoken in Europe. Some of these these languages are English, Dutch, Polish, Czech, French, Hungarian, Icelandic, and Spanish. Religion is an important part of life for many Europeans. Most Europeans are Christians. However, many Jewish and Muslim people also live on the continent. About 60 percent of Europeans live in cities. Many others live in towns or small villages. Europe's largest cities are Paris, Moscow, London, and Milan.

This little girl lives in the Netherlands. People who live in the Netherlands speak Dutch.

17

European Industry

The Industrial Revolution started in Europe in the late 1700s. During that time, European **manufacturers**, or people who make goods, began using power-driven machinery to produce their products. Soon people around the world began to make large numbers of goods at cheaper prices. Today Europe produces many manufactured goods. They include cars, chemicals, medicines, clothing, and electronics. **Agriculture** is an important European **industry**. Farmers grow crops, including corn, oats, potatoes, and wheat. They also raise animals, such as cows, goats, pigs, and sheep. Near the European coast, the fishing industry is very big.

18

Germany is a world leader in manufacturing automobiles. ▶

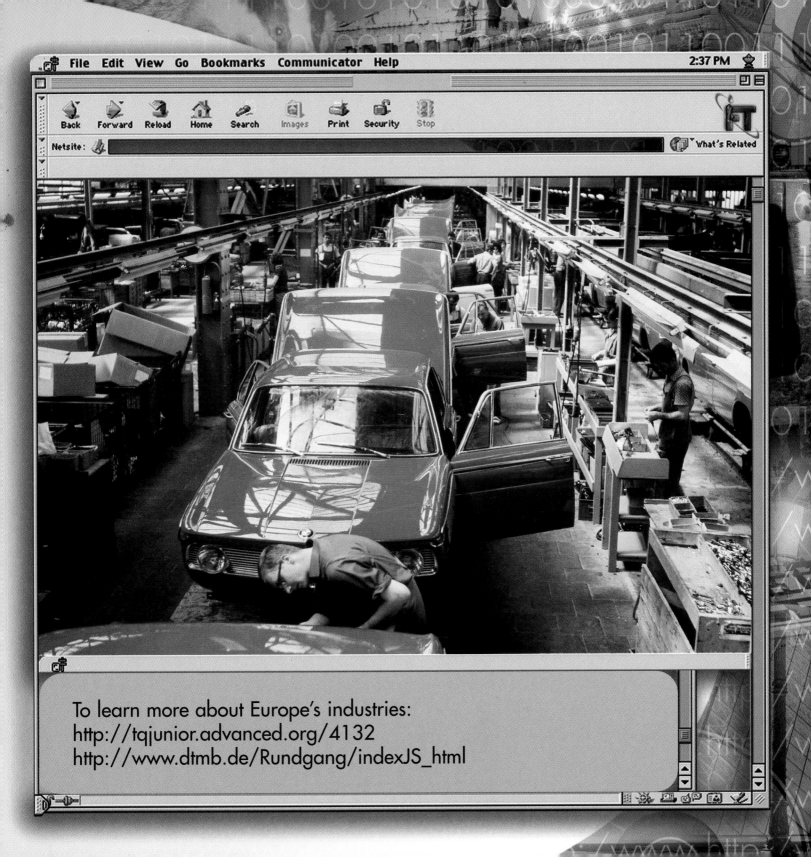

To learn more about Europe's industries:
http://tqjunior.advanced.org/4132
http://www.dtmb.de/Rundgang/indexJS_html

To learn more about European art:
http://www.kfki.hu/~arthp/index.html
http://www.hermitage.ru/

A Rich Artistic Tradition

Europe has produced some of the most famous art in the world! Much of the world's well-known literature and music was created by Europeans. William Shakespeare, the most famous **playwright** of all time, was from Great Britain. Beethoven and Bach are among history's most talented **composers** of music. **Opera** started in Europe, particularly in Italy and Germany.

Painting, sculpture, and dance also have rich European **traditions**. Michelangelo, an Italian painter and sculptor, is one of the world's most famous artists. European **architecture** has produced some amazing buildings, including castles, churches, and cathedrals.

◀ *You can find many of the world's most important museums in Europe. This photo shows the Louvre museum in Paris.*

Back   Forward   Reload   Home   Search   Images   Print   Security   Stop

Netsite: What's Related

Let's Learn More!

Europe is one of the most interesting and exciting places to visit. It is a continent filled with lots of different groups of people, each with its own language, art, and way of life. From weather and **geography**, to animals and people, to art and industry, Europe is a unique place. Life in Europe has affected the way people live all over the world. Do you want to know more about how this has happened? Well, keep surfing. The answers to all your questions about Europe are out there, on the Internet! To learn more about life in European countries, go to:
http://www.geographia.com/indx03.htm

agriculture (AH-grih-kuhl-cher) Farming.

architecture (AR-kih-tek-cher) The work of designing and constructing buildings.

canals (ka-NALS) Bodies of water that are usually narrow.

climate (KLY-mit) The kind of weather a certain area has.

composers (kom-POHZ-erz) People who write and create music.

continents (KON-tin-ents) The seven great masses of land on Earth.

extinct (ik-STINKT) To no longer exist.

geography (jee-AH-gruh-fee) The study of Earth's surface, climate, continents, countries, and people.

industry (IN-des-tree) A business that makes a product or provides a service.

landmass (LAND-mas) A very large area of land.

manufacturers (man-yoo-FAK-cher-erz) People who make something by hand or with a machine.

opera (AH-prah) A stage play that is sung to music.

playwright (PLAY-ryt) A person who writes plays.

population (pop-yoo-LAY-shun) The number of people who live in a region.

traditions (truh-DIH-shunz) Ways of doing something that are passed down through the years.

Index

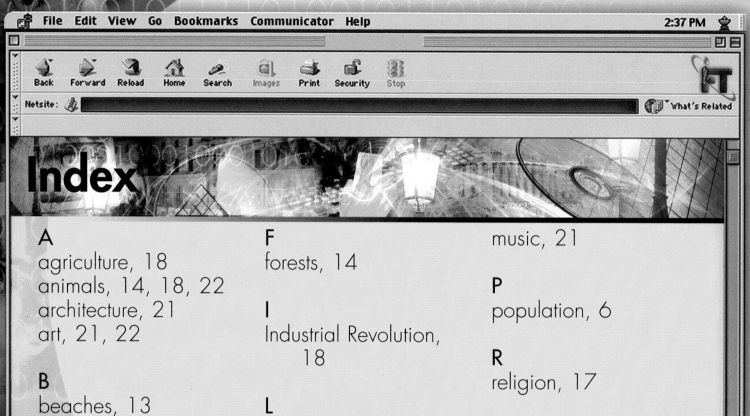

Web Sites

Check out the exciting Web sites about Europe on these pages:
pp. 7, 8, 11, 12, 15, 16, 19, 20, and 22.

24